Captain Billy's
Whiz Bang

Ame
W

FEBRUARY, 1922   Vol. III.   No. 30

Published
Monthly **W. H. Fawcett,** at Robbinsdale,
Rural Route No. 2   Minnesota

Entered as second-class matter May, 1, 1920, at the postoffice at
Robbinsdale, Minnesota, under the
Act of March 3, 1879.

Price 25 cents   **$2.50 per year**
ONE DOLLAR FOR THE WINTER ANNUAL

"We have room for but one soul loyalty and that is loyalty to the American people.—Theodore Roosevelt.

Captain Billy's Whiz Bang employs no solicitors. Subscriptions may be received only at authorized news stands or by direct mail to Robbinsdale. We join in no clubbing offers, nor do we give premiums. Two–fifty a year in advance.

Edited by a Spanish and World War Veteran and dedicated to the fighting forces of the United States

2008 edition published by About Comics,
Thousand Oaks, California
www.AboutComics.com
For bulk purchase information, email
sales@aboutcomics.com
ISBN: 0-9790750-3-3
ISBN-13: 978-0-9790750-3-2
PRINTED IN CANADA

Drippings From the Fawcett

Gentle readers, wet your lips, for whilst with dry tongues thou art yearning, your obedient servant, Bilious Billy, is in the land of liberty—personal and otherwise—basking in Cuba's sunny clime, in Havana, sucking soda through a straw! Soda! Sure, soda with a dash in it. When we grow tired of fast horses and saintly senoritas, it will be back again to the big pines of northern Minnesota for the fishing season at Breezy Point Lodge. You know, folk, in the winter we Minnesotans can't fish, as our Norwegian friends would say.

* * *

WELL, boys and girls, here I am on the road again—just like a wandering Jew. In making my present departure from Robbinsdale, I didn't know whether I was coming to Montreal or going to Cuba.

The high cost of coal in Robbinsdale made me long for summer at Miami Beach, where there is no charge for hot rolls in the sand and a little chicken nearby. Then again I was reminded of having seen Willie and Mollie playing in the sand, indulging in youthful folly. The sand was terribly hot on Willie's back and the sun was hot tamale.

Woke up in Chicago with an ice-pack attached to my fevered brow, and appreciating that the United States is the land of personal liberty I hied forth towards Miami to see if I might not be able to obtain a "wee snifter." Miami is now the legal home of William Jennings Bryan and I did not have much luck in satisfying an unquenchable thirst. Anyway, if I did, it wouldn't be nice to tell about. Mr. Bryan may have something to do with keeping Miami and the State of Florida bone-dry— which it isn't—so more power to him. Florida may be dry, but in the unmortal words of our snuff-chewing hired man, I am pleased to report that there are a lot of "damp rascals" here.

Understand the Floridians are seriously considering Bryan for United States Senator. Had the pleasure today of driving through the backyard of the Commoner's palatial home, but all I could see was the rear door and his smoke-house. Mr. Bryan was too busy addressing a Baptist convention to even invite me to lunch. Tomorrow he is slated for a Bible talk in the city park and if I get up in time, and feel all right, shall listen to his discourse. (Later, didn't get up in time.)

                           * * *

AFTER leaving Chicago I stopped at Atlanta for a few days' sojourn. Here we struck nice warm sunshine. The Atlanta ladies are a genial lot, but their costuming somewhat crashes with the constitutional scheme of affairs as laid down by the eighteenth amendment. Their hats are full of cocktails—and sometimes also their heads, I am told. In fact, a bird of paradise plume is quite in vogue in Atlanta.

The information is also vouchsafed that some Atlanta girls are born foolish, while others marry.

Overheard a rather humorous remark of a local celebrity, Clayt Robson by name, one evening in the lobby of the Kimball house. Robson is a well-known Georgian lobbyist and political boss, who is considered a power in the present state administration. Clayt jokingly spluttered to a group of friends that "I was twenty-one years old and grown-up before I knew that 'damned Yankee' was two words."

My visit to Atlanta brought to memory a conversation I had with Cole S. Blease, former governor of South Carolina, about four years ago. The governor very kindly invited me to his suite in the Selwyn hotel at Charlotte, N. C., to partake of his private twenty-year-old stock. While "killing" the quart of medicine, the subject of Atlanta came to the front. Here is the Bleasian description of the South's largest city, as nearly as I can remember:

"Atlanta is a hell-hole of perdition. It is no place for a virtuous woman or an honest man."

I cannot quite agree with Mr. Blease, for Atlanta treated me royally. The girlies here I found to be of true Southern stock—very shy and rather demure. I once heard the late

"Pitchfork" Ben Tillman remark that the only family tree he could boast was that the women were virtuous and the men reasonably brave. From my cursory observations this description fairly fits Atlanta.

From Atlanta our next stop was Jacksonville. Went for a joyride here, which ended in a thrilling though harmless smashup. Upon picking myself from out the wreckage, I thanked the kindly doctor for a safe delivery. Which calls to mind these lines by Lincoln, or some other noted personage:

Oh why should the spirit of mortal be proud?
As he rides in his swift-flying car like a cloud,
A break in the axle, a bust in the tire,
He passeth from life to the heavenly choir.

* * *

AS A DEER hunter, I'm a good farmer. Spent ten days tramping the windfalls in the neighborhood of Breezy Point Lodge without even seeing a deer. Saw plenty of polecats, bobcats and house cats, and nearly captured a "porky." I learned lots about the habits and habitations of the northern pine animals and finally managed to knock down a "spike buck" (whatever that means) on the last day of the hunting season. Must admit the buck almost shook hands with me before I was able to knock him over. However, I had a very good guide, Arthur Foote by name, but better known as "Panther Pete." Pete has earned a regular living for twenty-five years as a trap-

per and deer hunter, and I am sure that the
small buck never would have fallen for me had
he not enticed the animal to leave his forest
retreat.

* * *

WHILE touring the San Francisco under-
world as the guest of the police vice
squad on my recent tour of the Pacific
coast, we encountered what the police considered a suspicious party.

He was one of those dapper young men with
a red necktie that frequent this section of
Famous Frisco.

"What's your occupation?" asked one of the
policemen of the young man.

"I'm a business man," was the answer as the
young man started to trip blithely away.

"Wait a minute," said the cop. "I never saw
a business man walk like that."

"Oh," replied the dapper youth, "but you
don't know what kind of business I'm in!"

Thirty days for him.

* * *

DURING my recent rampage about the
American continent it was my pleasure
to appreciate the service of Tiajuana,
and I could not resist the temptation to con-
trast this Mexican village with the Canadian
metropolis, Montreal. In Montreal I enjoyed
a bottle of Pom Roger champagne without being a law breaker, even though it cost me ten
cents for a two by four sandwich. From Mon-

treal I hustled to the deer hunting regions of
northern Minnesota and found no champagne
or other imported wines, but plenty of "mountain dew." With all due respect to Mr. Andrew
J. Volstead, our Minnesota congressman, there
is today in this grand and glorious land of the
free and home of the brave more rotten booze
than it was ever my lot to drink in the pre-
prohibition days.

But to get back to my deer hunting expedi-
tion, I must admit that the deer were scarce
but—

> *But there were polecats and goosehawks,*
> *And a four-legged cow;*
> *Wild pigs and wild boars,*
> *And a thing like a sow.*
> *There were thousands of screech owls,*
> *Turkey buzzards and quail,*
> *And a little black jack-ass*
> *With a damnable tail,*
> *With their foll de dol dol*
> *And fol de dol day.*

* * *

WHILE flivvering out near Golden Valley,
Minnesota, I dropped in at the farm of
my old friend, John Foss, to pass the
time of day. I noticed a drove of hogs on his
timber lot acting peculiar. They would run
up to a tree and squeal like mad, then leave
that tree and go to another and do the same
thing, continuing in their mad scamper around
the timber lot.

"What makes them act that way?" I asked John.

"Well," replied old man Foss, "last winter I had a throat infection and lost the power of speech for a month or more and couldn't call them to their feed, so I taught them to come by rapping on a post or a tree, and now the darn woodpeckers are setting them crazy."

* * *

AT Breezy Point Lodge I have an old gray mare and I love to sing this melody of my boyhood days:

> The old gray mare
> She sits on the single tree,
> Sits on the whipple tree,
> Sits on the single tree.

And, believe me, her greatest indoor and outdoor sport is sitting on the single tree.

* * *

UP IN the deer hunting grounds of northern Minnesota the jack-pine savages are still singing that old familiar ditty about the much maligned bird—the woodpecker. These heart throbbing words peal gently through the evening air:

> "I stuck my finger in a woodpecker's hole,
> And the woodpecker said: 'Gosh darn your soul,'
> 'Take it out; take it out; take it out; take it out.'"

* * *

THE other day I was riding on a street car in Minneapolis. Sitting opposite me was a very pretty young lady who had a poodle dog in her lap. Bluenose lady sitting next to the girl addressed her thusly: "My, what a nasty little dog. Don't you think, my young lady, it would look much nicer if you had a little baby in your lap?"

"No," the pretty one replied in calm even tones, "it wouldn't. You see I'm not married."

* * *

CHIEF BLOBERGER surveyed a party of hoboes coming down the Great Northern tracks.

"Here they come, hog fat and crummy, short pipes and red noses. Won't work, ain't allowed to shoot 'em, and if you don't feed 'em they'll burn your barn daown."

* * *

Extra! Extra!

Ladies and gentlemen: Don't fail to be in Robbinsdale next Tuesday at four o'clock A. M. to witness the daring feat of Peter, our hired man. This brave snoosegrinding son of toil will endeavor to dive off the top of the highest building in Robbinsdale into a six-foot tank of solid concrete, playing the ukelele, eating raw liver and keeping perfect time. The spectacular dive by Pete will be for a worthy cause. All proceeds from the entertainment will be donated to the starving plumbers of Chicago. Admission free.

* * *

TOOK my wife into a store to assist her in buying a new hat. Like all women, she tried on nearly every hat in the store. In desperation the salesman appealed to me with this remark: "How would you like me to try a sailor for your wife?" Having been in the army for many years, I felt like suggesting a soldier, for this insulting salesman. Needless to say, the sale was not made.

* * *

ON MY recent visit to New York I had the pleasure of the company of Mr. H. A. D'Arcy, author of "The Face Upon the Floor," which we misnamed in past issues "The Face Upon the Barroom Floor." This masterpiece undoubtedly stands first among popular present day poems, judging from the many requests we received from Whiz Bang readers for its republication. To Ye Editor Mr. D'Arcy told the history of how "The Face Upon the Floor" was inspired:

"Away back in the early 80's Union Square in New York was called 'The Rialto' agreeable to the fact that it was the theatrical center of America. On the corner of Fourth avenue and Fourteenth street, a very excellent saloon was run by Joe Schmidt and it was kept fairly full from noon to midnight with respectable members of the sock and buskin, and amusement promoters. One Saturday evening in August, 1887, a table in front of the bar was occupied by a bunch of managers. We were combining business with pleasure, booking time and enjoying the very excellent beer and spirits available in those happy days. It was probably about 11 o'clock when a mendicant shambled in and approached our table. With a sad, husky voice, he said, 'Gentlemen, I want a drink.' All eyes were turned to the derelict and someone at the table offered one of the untasted glasses of whisky which was quickly swallowed. Joe behind the bar yelled, 'Get out.'

"The waiter in front quickly seized the beggar and threw him out of the swinging door; to make the situation more dramatic, a rough haired terrier dog named 'Toby' and pet of the saloon jumped at the poor devil and fastened on his pants. 'Toby' always thought it his duty to chase poor people, and had an innate antipathy to jumpers or pants not duly pressed.

"Well, several of the party got up from the table and went out to see what had happened to the poor wretch. He was lying on the sidewalk with his face halfway in the gutter. We gathered him up, brushed him off a little, wiped his face and someone went into the saloon and brought out another drink of whisky. Several coins were carefully dropped into the inside pocket of his coat. This was done surreptitiously so that he would not know the money was there until the tomorrow. As we left him on a door step next door I asked what his trade was and he managed to tell me he was an artist. I held that this man was not a professional beggar, a derelict true, but probably had once been a talented man. The argument was taken up by several other gentlemen in the room and waxed warm until I got angry and with a curt "good night" bolted out of the saloon. On my way home, I determined to write up the story in such a way as would make my argument good and satisfy Joe Schmidt that I was not wholly chicken-hearted. I also was pretty sure of winning the fair hostess to my way of thinking. As I walked along I composed in my mind the first two lines:

"*'Twas a balmy summer evening and a goodly crowd was there,*
That well-nigh filled Joe's bar-room on the corner of the Square."

"The measure was a happy iambic tetrameter and fitted the story, and before going to bed, I jotted down the first two lines which I have always found the hardest to compose, next day I finished the story. When Joe read it, I saw tears in his eyes. It was published in the New York Dispatch. Joe bought a hundred copies of the paper and sent 25 to the Buffalo Bill Co. who were playing in London and among whom both he and I had many friends. Cody and Major Burke circulated the copies among their theatrical friends and before many months three vaudevillians were reciting the poem at the big music halls, then Sam Bernard set America crazy with it and yet after over thirty years, it is still a popular 'act' and wins excellent booking.

"I have been often told that my story set the pace for prohibition. I sincerely hope not. If I thought that I had helped that unfortunate law, I would walk down to the dock and kick myself into the river. 'The Face Upon the Floor' is not a temperance story, but an admonition to the world, not to despise the unfortunate derelict."

In this issue we are pleased to publish another poem by Mr. D'Arcy and have his promise of more to follow. And let me add, I found Mr. D'Arcy a regular fellow, well met, an excellent conversationalist and a fine reminder of the good old days.

* * *

GUS, our ex-hired man, escorted a petite young lady to her apartment.

"Just as I was putting my arm around her," Gus reports, "a man walked in."

"My gawsch, my husband!" exclaimed the girl.

"Oh, busy honey?" the intruder remarked, as he walked out.

* * *

OUR new hired man, Ikey, from the cities, is so absentminded that when he went in the stable to saddle a horse, he was surprised to find, after a half hour's work, that he

had the saddle on himself and he spent another
half hour in vain trying to climb on his own
back.

* * *

The Wa-hoo-wa Bird

Ladies and Gentlemen, I take great pleasure in pre-
senting to you the Wa-hoo-wa Bird. The only bird of
its kind in captivity today. This strange bird comes from
the far off shores of the Isle of Borneo where it rears its
young among the crannies and crags of the mountainous
coastline. Now the particular strange thing about this
bird is that it only mates once every one hundred years,
and after having mated, it crawls, half drags, half flies,
until it gets itself to the topmost pinnacle of the long,
tall, lofty rubber tree. Casting its eyes to the heavens it
cries in tones of ecstacy "Wa-hoo-wa," which, translated
in the language of the natives, means "My Gawsch,
Mamma, ain't love grand!"

* * *

Deciding the Race

Pat and Mike were to run a race to a tree
by different routes.

Pat—"If oi get there first oi'll make a mark
on the tree with this chalk, Mike, and if you
get there first you rub it off."

* * *

The Old Boy's Chatter

The fellow who marries a bow-legged girl
these days has no excuse that he can't see what
he's getting.

* * *

He doesn't dress so neat on work days, but
he wears his new hat on his week end.

This Bends in the Middle

Santa Claus played a dirty trick on the bow-legged girls, didn't he?

Why?

See what he put in their stockings!

* * *

Another Version of It

No matter how pretty a bow-legged girl may be; she is always in bad shape.

* * *

Did you ever go to the postoffice to attend the graduation exercises of a correspondence school class?

* * *

The Charity Bazaar

"How much am I offered for this pie?" sang out the auctioneer.

"Six bits," one youth bid.

"Who will make it eighty? Just imagine, you get the girl and all!"

"Say, mister," ejaculated the youth, "what kind of pie is it you're selling?"

* * *

Shed Tears, Brothers

Yep, I've quit th' holdup game,
I'll hang 'round joints no more.
So with a sigh
And a faint little cry
The garter stretched out on the floor!

* * *

Our Monthly Maxim

A bell's a bell even though it is on a cow.

Our Monthly Toast

For fill up your glasses,
And fill 'em up full,
And drink to the health
Of the Pedigreed Bull.

* * *

Indoor Sports
(From "The Blue Lagoon," a novel.)

Her ears were small and like little white shells. He would take one between finger and thumb and play with it as if it were a toy, pulling at the lobe of it or trying to flatten out the curved part. Her breasts, her shoulders, her knees, her little feet, every bit of her, he would examine and play with and kiss. She would lie and let him, seeming absorbed in some far-away thought, of which he was the object; then all at once her arms would go round him. All this used to go on in the broad light of day, under the shadow of the artu leaves, with no one to watch except the bright-eyed birds in the leaves above.

* * *

Not In Robbinsdale

Hello, is this the chief of the Fire Department?

Yes, this is the chief.

Well, my house is on fire.

How long has it been burnin'?

Half hour.

Did you try puttin' water on it?

Yes, but it won't go out.

Then 'taint no use in us comin' over, because that's all we could do. G'Bye!

* * *

Women are the greatest edition in the world and no man should be without a copy.

Parlor Story

A southern restaurant serves eggs with all meat orders. A patron ordered pork chops.

"Boss, how do yo' all want yo' eggs," inquired the waiter.

"Oh, you can eliminate the eggs."

The waiter repeated the order to the colored chef and added "liminate dem eggs."

The chef scratched his head. "Sambo, yo tell dat customer ah ain't got no time this mawning to liminate dem eggs and that he all will have to have dem cooked some oder way."

* * *

Speaking About Atrocities

The occupants of the parlor car of the limited were startled by the abrupt entrance of two masked bandits. "T'row up yer hands," commanded the bigger of the two. "We're gonna rob all the gents and kiss all the gals."

"No, pardner," responded the smaller one gallantly, "We'll rob all the gents but we'll leave the ladies alone."

"Mind your own business, young fellow," snapped a female passenger of uncertain age, "The big man's robbing this train."

* * *

Pat's Practical Piety

The ice in the river was thin as Pat started to "feel" his way across. Every time Pat put down his right foot he muttered reverently "Praise the Lord," and as the left foot hit the thin ice, "The devil ain't such a bad man."

At the other side of the river, Pat, with a sigh of relief, turned back and said "Tuhel with both of yez."

Useless Effort

Paddy Ryan in Ireland inherited a pile of money and decided to tour France. He hired a guide who steered him up a mountain. After a full day's climb they reached the summit.

"See ze beautiful valley," said the guide to Paddy, pointing below.

"Sure," stormed the Irishman, "if it's so dom beautiful in the valley what the divil for did you bring me 'way up here?"

* * *

And He Got It

"You are working too hard," said a policeman to a man who was drilling a hole in a safe at 2:00 o'clock in the morning.

"What do you mean?" asked the burglar in a disconcerted tone.

"I mean you need arrest," answered the policeman.

* * *

It Rained Keys, Bo!

I met a wonderful girl yesterday afternoon, and she invited me up to her apartment. That night she told me to stand in front of the door and whistle three times and she would throw down the key.

Boys, I never saw so many keys in all my life.

* * *

I could print a lot of real funny stories, but what's the use, you would only laugh at them.

Questions and Answers

Dear Capt. Billy—What is the first thing that turns green in the spring?—*Uppan Attim.*

Christmas jewelry.

* * *

Dear Captun: My kid brother's a great chicken chaser. He came home late last night all dizzy; d'you think he was drinkin' or what's the matter?—*Ida Sinkey.*

'Swimmin' in the head.

* * *

Dear Whiz Bang Bill—Is there much food values in dates?—*Ona Dyett.*

It all depends on who you make them with.

* * *

Dear Captain—What is a Sly Oodle?—*Nat. U. List.*

'Tis a small weasel that sleeps in the crotch of a tree, and swallows its nose to keep it from freezing.

* * *

Dear Capt. Billy—A fellow asked me a funny question the other day. Why is a crow? Seems sort of silly. Do you know the answer? —*M. T. Kann.*

That's easy. Caws.

Dear Captain Billy—What is a Nabisco?—*Ray Vaughan.*

It consists of two pieces of tissue paper with a little honey between.

* * *

Dear Captain Billy—Would it hurt me to sleep between two windows?—*I. Foozle.*

You would have a "pane" on the chest and back, and a "catch" on your side.

* * *

Dear Capt. Billy—What is a good name for a new college sorority?—*Al E. Wrat.*

I. Phelta Thi.

* * *

Dear Capt. Billy—What is a sculptor?—*Cant E. Lope.*

A man that makes faces and busts.

* * *

Dear Capt. Billy—What is dust?—*Hose Ette.*

Mud with the juice squeezed out.

* * *

Dear Capt. Billy—Is hair tonic a good drink?—*J. Fewbrains.*

Would advise you not to drink hair tonic as it will raise a mustache on your appendix and if you should laugh you would tickle yourself to death.

* * *

Dear Farmer Bill—Please inform me where milk comes from.—*A City Girl.*

From cow faucets.

Dear Capt. Billy—If my father was a duke and my mother was a duchess, what would that make me?—*Watts D. Yoos.*

Why, I guess you would be Duke's Mixture.

* * *

Dear Captain—Tell me something interesting about auction bridge.—*Adeline Moore.*

All we know about is Brooklyn Bridge, and that is just one long suspense.

* * *

Dear Capn.—What did my beau mean when he told me he would meet me in the future?—*Sarah Desert.*

Probably he meant in the pasture.

* * *

Dear Capt. Billy—What is a drydock?—*Torchy.*

A physician who won't give us prescriptions.

* * *

The Farm That Bull Built

Oh! over the hill to Robbinsdale,
For a slap on the back and a hearty hail.
Where the cows do tricks in the new mown hay,
And the Bull is thrown in a very quaint way.

Where Gus is tired from morn till night,
And the old silo is always tight.
Where the chickens sing and the roosters crow.
And the corn does a hoe-down row on row.

So up the road to the Whiz Bang farm
Where the onions grow but do no harm.
It's a merry crowd that slings the hoe
On Billy's farm. Come gang let's go.

* * *

They tell me people are so tough in South St. Paul they play Tiddly-Winks with the sewer covers. Zatright?

Fable of a Poodle

Once there was a guy who wished that he was a rich woman's lap-dog, when suddenly a Great Genii appeared before him and granted his wish, telling him that any time he wished to be changed back to a man, he should slip out of the rich lady's house and come to the home of the Genii, in a distant part of the city.

Being only a dog, he soon grew tired of his pampered life, and since he was really a dog, the kisses and petting of his pretty mistress failed to produce the "kick" that he had anticipated.

So, he slipped out of the house, and found himself on a broad and spacious avenue, lined with trees, telegraph poles and iron fence posts.

Now, that was many moons ago, but up to the present writing, the little doggie has not reached the Genii's house to be changed back to a man.

MORAL: It's a poor wish that won't work two ways.

* * *

French Proverbs
(Selected by Rev. G. L. Morrill.)

Women give themselves to God when the Devil wants nothing more to do with them.

Since Cupid is represented with a torch in his hand, why did they place virtue on a barrel of gunpowder?

A woman forgives everything but the fact that you do not covet her.

Fools never understand people of wit.

Outside the Show

"Hello, Bill, how did you enjoy the show last night?"

"Fine, Joe. Wasn't that some pippin in the bathing suit?"

"Yep, Bill!"

"Well, I saw her without the suit on today."

!!!!!_____(street clothes?)

* * *

Familiarity Breeds Contempt

John Philip Sousa traveled six thousand miles to hear the celebrated chimes of an English church. As he was drawing near the place the wonderful chimes rang out, and enraptured, Sousa exclaimed to the driver of the vehicle, "You folk are indeed fortunate to live within sound of those heavenly chimes.

"I can't hear a word you say," shouted the driver irritably," them d—— bells deafen me."

* * *

As You Were

Sexton—"Dogs are not allowed here, sir."

Visitor—"That's not my dog."

Sexton—"Not your dog? Why, he's following you."

Visitor—"Well, so are you."

* * *

We Pull Lots of These

A cross-eyed man at a dance hall said "May I have the next dance, please?" Two girls answered as with one voice, "With pleasure."

That Reminds Me

Algernon—Dearest, I could sit here forever gazing into your charming eyes and listening to the wash of the ocean.

The Girl—That reminds me, Honey. I have a laundry bill and I'm dead broke.

* * *

There's one thing I can't eat for breakfast and that is supper.

* * *

While a darky was being led to the gallows a crowd of people ran past him.

"What yo all running fo?" yelled Sambo after them, "Dey ain't nothin' gwine to happen till ah gets dere."

* * *

He is so stingy he goes to the postoffice to fill his fountain pen.

* * *

April Fool

Johnny (running into the room of his mother on April 1st)—"Mama, there's a strange man kissing our maid."

Mother—"What, a strange man?"

Johnny—"April fool, it's only papa."

* * *

Curbstone Comedy

He stopped the balky car.

"Honey, I must get out and spank the engine over the ears."

"Oh, engine-ears!"

We Pass

The nurse at the front regarded the wounded soldier with a puzzled look.

"Your face is familiar to me, but I can't place you," she said.

"Let bygones be bygones, baby," replied the soldier, "I used to be a policeman."

* * *

Riddle-de-doot!

Where did you get that rose?
That isn't a rose, that's a geranium,
No, it isn't. It's a rose.
I said it's a geranium.
How do you spell it?
It's a rose all right.

* * *

My girl has Pullman teeth.
One upper and one lower.

* * *

Colorado Springs is sure some town. Had to go up to the city hall to get a permit from the mayor to play a game of dominoes.

* * *

This wash board is a hundred years old.
Yes, it surely is wrinkled.

* * *

Punctuation

"Men are naturally grammatical."
"Yes?"
"When they see an abbreviated skirt they always look after it for a period."

Chalk Up One Error

Chicago.—Mrs. R. Kelly sat watching a thrilling movie. Without taking her eyes off the film, she landed an uppercut on the jaw of the man sitting next to her. "I must have made a mistake," Jake Cohen told the judge. "I didn't know I put my hand on her knee!"

* * *

Remember This One?

The first scene is that of a gambler,
Who has lost all his money at play;
Takes his dead mother's ring from her finger
Which she wore on her wedding day,
His last earthly treasure he stakes it
Bows his head the shame he may hide.
When they raised up his head,
They found he was dead
'Tis a picture from life's other side.

* * *

"Say, Mr. Jones, what do you want to get married for?"

"Because I don't want my name to die out."

* * *

"You don't love me any more,"
She sobbed and bowed her head.
"What tuhel's the difference,"
The villainous rascal said.

* * *

A cat, mistaking a ball of wool for a meat ball, swallowed it, and sure enough when she had kittens they had on sweaters.

* * *

Child's is a great place to eat. Went in there yesterday and amongst the dirty dishes on the table I found thirty cents.

Movie Hot Stuff

THESE be dull days in the movie and even the stage world. The dark clouds of the Arbuckle case still hang over the two "arts," thanks to the obdurate lady juror who caused a disagreement in the San Francisco trial. The pleasantly informal old days, when Wallie Reid could run up to 'Frisco and pelt eggs upon pedestrians from the fourteenth floor of the St. Francis Hotel, are long past. One simply *has* to be circumspect these days.

After Whiz Bang's comments upon the way the New York stage was getting away with salaciousness came a police investigation of "The Demi-Virgin," the gentle whimsy with the strip poker game. The farce was severely condemned by the police commissioner—but it is still running and to crowded houses. The risque plays have had one or two additions since we wrote last.

For instance, there's David Belasco's adaptation of the French farce, "Kiki," with a little gutter gamin of the French music hall as its heroine. Mr. Belasco has substituted the word marriage for liason throughout but the intent is there—and the lines, oh, boy! Once Kiki remarks "The men are like cats—they follows us as though our veins were full of catnip!" Then there is a whole act in which Kiki—posing as a rigid somnambulist—is carried and tossed about by the various members of the cast, all the time dressed only in a simple pair of open work pajamas.

We aren't intimating that "Kiki" isn't entertaining. It is. But, the latitude they get away with! Meanwhile the censors go on cutting out bathing girls from our films and making sure there is no indication ever shown that babies are born.

* * *

CHARLIE RAY, spats, cane, trick overcoat with its fur collar, et al., has been making his first visit to New York and not creating a ripple of interest. Of course, friend wife was along. We saw Ray strolling up Fifth Avenue the other day—and nobody knew the ornate pedestrian as the simple country boy of the films. They tell me that Ray takes himself very seriously and left the cynical New York reporters dizzy with his confessions about his "mission in life."

* * *

JACK PICKFORD continues to loiter about New York. There are all sorts of rumors linking Jack up with pretty Marilyn Miller o' the Follies. Marilyn lost her husband, Frank Carter, in an auto accident some time ago and is as pleasant a little widow as the White

Lights possess. Maybe Marilyn has an eye towards the screen. By the way, those reports of an impending family event in the Fairbanks family still persists. What could be nicer?

*   *   *

POOR ERIC VON STROHEIM! We sympathize with him despite his Junker physiognomy. He is telling sad tales of his treatment at the hands of Universal. After finishing "Foolish Wives," they took the negative away from him, hired somebody or other to cut it—and Eric came on to New York to find out where he stood.

At last reports he is still trying to find out. Overheard him in a hotel recently telling his troubles. Now and then a tear splashed in the soup. You see, they have taken his brain child —his masterpiece—away and are letting some cruel inartistic outsider cut it any old way. It seems that Carl Laemmle, prexy of Universal, became irate over the way "Foolish Wives" cost money and never seemed to finish. Eric says they put all sorts of obstructions in his way. They locked cutting room doors, held up his pet plans, and all that, according to Eric. Finally —whisper, for it may only be a pipe dream— Eric organized and armed his army of extras after the fashion of Mr. William Hohenzollern and presented an ultimatum. He got what he wanted. Pause to consider the news story that nearly came out of Universal. Suppose Eric had cut the communication wires, tried military gas on the officials and made the studio into an armed camp. It sounds fishy, of course, but have you ever met the tense Mr. Von Stroheim?

At that we feel awfully sorry for him. He *has* unusual directorial ability and he is—or was—the one able person at Universal. And now, after making "Foolish Wives," which, if it doesn't get barred by the censors, ought to be a whirlwind, he seems to be getting the gate.

* * *

AREN'T those morality clauses the high minded movie producers are inserting into their actor contracts the bunk? Imagine the nerve. Will Rogers gave the best summary when he declared, "Say, if any one hands me a contract with one of them clauses, I'll say, you sign it first." He is in New York doing a turn on the Ziegfeld roof. The best line of his act is: "I'm the only guy who ever went to California and came back with the same wife."

* * *

ONE of the funniest kick backs from the Arbuckle case occurred at Vitagraph, where they had Maclyn Arbuckle (no relation to Fatty), under contract to be co-starred in "The Prodigal Judge," which he had played for years on the stage. Just as the picture was completed, a little San Francisco scandal broke. Vitagraph decided that it couldn't afford to feature Mr. Maclyn *Arbuckle* at this time. This despite the fact that Mr.

Maclyn was a well known star before Fatty was ever heard of. But luckily he had a sense of humor. So he said, "Oh, well (maybe it wasn't exactly that), you can't buck such reasoning," and let his name go into tiny type.

* * *

Very Well

I said she'd made with me a hit—
    Very well.
Perhaps I was a trifle lit—
    Very well.
I told her that she was divine,
She let me hold her hand in mine,
In short—I handed out my line
    Very well.

I whispered softly in her ear,
    Very well.
'Twas, how appropriately! dear—
    Very well.
I drew her snugly to my breast,
While she, not daring to protest
Cleaned out the pockets of my vest.
    Very well.

* * *

A Tough Steak

Cannibal No. 1—What makes the chief such a bunk spreader?

Cannibal No. 2—He just ate the editor of Whiz Bang.

* * *

Nah, Nah!

"Is my wife forward?" asked the passenger on the Limited.

"She wasn't to me sir," answered the conductor politely.

Whiz Bang **Editorials**

"The Bull is Mightier Than the Bullet."

H ATS off to a real man of the cloth. The Rev. D. H. Jones has resigned the pulpit of Huntington Park, California, Baptist Church, because of the fanatical attempts of his flock to enforce Sunday closing.

"I prefer to dwell with the worldling and be true to my inner self than to live with the saint and betray it," Reverend Jones says.

"There is a way to make the church the super-attraction; but it will never be done by coercing the consciences of men. The Cross of Christ is proving to be the greatest magnet in the world, but use it as a club, and it will become a colossal failure."

"Killed professionally, yes. But, frankly, I would rather be a man than a minister. Character is greater than profession."

"I would just as soon believe that the perfume of the rose comes from the polecat as to believe that the spirit of the blue laws comes from God."

"Christ whipped men out of the church, but never into it. 'Profesional reformers' and 'Christian lobbyists' at Washington may mean well, but most of them are misguided swivel-chair heroes of the Cross."

"'Close every door except the church's,' cries the reformer, forgetting that open hearts are greater induce-ments than closed doors."

"The doctrine behind the blue laws is this: 'I am in

the right and you are in the wrong. When you are stronger than I, you ought to tolerate; for it is your duty to tolerate truth. But when I am the stronger, I shall persecute you; for it is my duty to persecute error.' "

"All the proposed Sunday legislation is simply a human attempt to whitewash what God designed to wash white. To condemn movies because some things may be objectionable is like refusing to eat fish because it contains bones."

"When human passion is subdued, when the turbulent tide ebbs, we see that the big thing that lies at the bottom of the opposition of theatre opening on Sunday, is simply bigotry."

"It is a wonder to me how many bad things good people see in the movies; fortunately, if you are so disposed, you need never be disappointed. The product of a legal religion has ever been and ever will be either hypocricy or persecution."

* * *

A LITTLE white coffin rested on a small table, covered with flowers white as the waxen face and fair hair of the baby child whose short life of thirteen months' suffering was ended.

A small company of kind neighbors was present. The clergyman repeated the Saviour's words, "Suffer the children to come unto me and forbid them not, for of such is the kingdom of heaven," and told how the little life had not paid in dollars and cents, but that judged by an immortal existence begun here, and to last forever, Death was gain. After the father, sisters and brothers said "Good-bye," the mother took the last farewell kiss of her baby and baptized it anew with her hot falling tears. So small was the casket that the undertaker lifted it in his arms, just as the mother had the sick child, and carried it to the carriage and placed it on the seat.

We entered the beautiful green cemetery, and lowered the little flower-decked coffin in the grave to rest until God's "Good morning" in the graveless, griefless home of heaven. As I looked back, the mound seemed so small that a child could step over it in his play, but I knew it was higher than a mountain top to the mother because in it was buried all her love and hope.

So we left the little casket and the little body in the little grave, feeling that this bud of promise would be transplanted to the Eternal Garden where the full flower would blossom and bloom without decay.

*   *   *

THE Detroit Free-Press calls it the "Snoopers' Brigade," and we are inclined to think that is a well-fitting title for the aggregation of people who are urging the formation of a society that would compel all men to be spies upon neighbors and reporters upon their actions.

Sometime ago a federal prohibition commissioner announced plans for such an association, but he immediately discovered that the people of the United States are not ready to become investigators of their neighbors' conduct, in any particular, and the project was squelched by higher authority.

The courts of the country are, very generally, excluding testimony obtained by men who lead others into the commission of crime, and properly; they regard such actions as a conspiracy to break the law, which makes the tempter a partner in the crime.

In a Mississippi case, where it appeared that a peace officer induced a man to purchase liquor for him and then arrested the man who succumbed to his blandishments, the judge ordered the accused discharged and the officer held. The official was subsequently convicted of his part in the crime, and the supreme court sustained the verdict against him.

There is a very general misapprehension on this subject and acts of the officials have been winked at because the public really did not know what was going on and did not realize the extent of the practice indulged in by what are very generally called stool pigeons.

The laws of this or any other state may be enforced without making all the people detectives, as the Snoopers' League would have them, or without permitting the practice of certain classes of officials, who sometimes literally hire men to commit a crime, in order that that very crime may be suppressed.

* * *

Where did I get my education? Why, me dad used to take me over his knee. He made me smart.

B ULLY for the Chicago Tribune. That journal slips the prong into Bluenose Crafts in a recent issue:

It is beginning to appear that the movement led by Mr. Crafts is as bigoted and as savage in its purpose as those which we thought were buried in the semi-barbarous past. It must be held that no human uplift but maniacal desire to inflict physical punishment is the motive. Mr. Crafts and his followers wish to put as many of their fellow countrymen as possible in jail, and they are trying to wreck this republic in order to do so.

* * *

Farmyard Notes

Chickens get tough when they run around too much.

* * *

Be it ever so humble, there's no flower like the cauli.

* * *

A bird in the oven is worth two in the bush and a berry in the bush is not worth two in the hand.

* * *

I wish I was cross-eyed, then I could stand on a windy day and gaze at a lady wearing a short skirt, right in the eye and still have a guilty conscience.

* * *

Cellar Ancestry

The potatoes eyes were full of tears,
And the cabbage hung its head,
For there was grief in the cellar that nite,
For the vinegar's mother was dead.

* * *

You can lead a cow to water but the Bull—he must be herd.

As It Is In New York

"On East Houston Street is the lasagne or ravioli belt where the gay boys from out of town take the leading ladies of the jobber plants out for a wild evening," writes O. O. McIntyre. "You know the gay out-of-town man. He carries a patent cigar lighter and has a sterling silver monogrammed belt buckle and, oh, yes, a handkerchief with a purple border. His eyes are blue and he wrinkles them in a merry twinkle, at least he thinks it is a merry twinkle, but it's just the sap oozing out. The Leading Lady knows Broadway because she reads Broadway Brevities and her theory of life in the abstract is that Ladies Must Live. After the first quart of red ink, he whispers a story the boys told him in front of the Bon Ton Store before he left for the east. She pulls the two gun, hair-trigger Bill Hart stuff and says 'Naughty Man.' To complete the evening and display the ultimate insavoir faire he calls loudly to the waiter: 'L'addition, s'il vous plait garcon.' They ride to one of the Oranges in a quick-firing metered taxi and he returns to the McAlpin to write the wife and kiddies of his lonesomeness."

* * *

New York

This is the old famous New York poem, credited to a former collector of the port as author, but denied. However, you'll note that every word carries a wallop and so we herewith, with your kind permission, republish it:

Vulgar of manner, overfed,
Over dressed, and underbred,
Heartless, Godless, hell's delight,
Rude by day, lewd by night,
Bedwarfed the man, enlarged the brute,
Ruled by Jew and prostitute
Purple robed and pauper clad
Raving, rioting, money mad—
A squirming herd of Mammon's mesh,
A wilderness of human flesh.
Crazed by avarice, lust and rum—
New York! Thy name's "Delirium."

Farm Life

"I see you are keeping your hired man all right now, Ezra."

"Yep, keeping him all right."

"He seems satisfied, too. How'd you do it?"

"Did everything he asked me to. Let him work only four hours and eat with the family. He got to complaining of dull evenings, so every night I give him the use of a car of his own, and the money to spend, to go to the movies in town."

"That ought to satisfy him."

"It didn't, though. He complained of his room, and so I coaxed my son to trade rooms with him. Then he seemed more settled like."

"I notice you've cut off your whiskers, Ezra."

"Yeah. Some more of that hired man's notions."

"How's that?"

"He complained they tickled him every time I kissed him good-night."

* * *

Wah, Wah!

"Golly, Moses! Dey got strawberries and cherries and all kinds o' fruit covered wit candy. What kind shall ah git?"

"Git a choc'lat covered watermillion."

* * *

Sic 'em, Tige!

"What you need is a tonic to sharpen your appetite," said the Doctor. "By the way, what is your occupation?"

"I am a sword swallower in a circus side-show," replied the caller.

* * *

Little Joe says, "They am jest as many sebbens on de dice as anything else, ony dey is bashfull."

Smokehouse Poetry

The greatest poem of the squared circle ever brought to light is in store for March Whiz Bang readers, "The Kid's Last Fight." That noted recitation of years ago has been obtained by the Whiz Bang, reset to verse, and will hold the boards in the March issue.

> *The way he staggered made me sick,*
> *I stalled, McGee yelled "cop him quick!"*
> *The crowd was wise and yellin' "fake,"*
> *They'd seen the chance I wouldn't take.*

* * *

"Chi Slim" Twangs 'is Bloomin' Lyre

By J. Eugene Chrisman.

Author of "Poppies," written exclusively for Captain Billy's Whiz Bang.

By the lake-front near Chicago with her elbows on her knee
There's a widder-woman waiting and I know she waits for me;
When the wind is from the stock-yards every odor seems to say
"Come you back you lost star-boarder, come you back you skunk and pay!"

Her apron it was greasy and her hair it hung in strings,
And her name was Sarah Lukens but it had been lots o' things!
When I saw her first a'diggin' up the makin's for a stew
And she wasn't wastin' nothing that a dog could chaw in two.
Blinkin' rough for me to lead, tooth-less, sallow and knock-knee'd
Wasn't carin' much for class tho—what I needed was a feed.

When the bunch had grabbed their hand-out and we had 'em on the go,
Then she'd start me for "Dutch" Ryan's with a two-bit piece to throw.
With her head upon my shoulder at the second growler full,
She was lonesome bo, that widder with the rough-stuff that she'd pull!

How I used to feed her full of the "mush-talk" and the bull
For the snow had begun blowin' and I didn't like to pull!

But that's all put behind me, long ago and far away
Since I hit out for St. Looey one night on the C. & A.
But they're tellin' in the jungles that the winter's one best bet
For a young and handsome hobo is to be a widder's pet.
Oh them boardin' kitchen smells as she fed me jams and jells
And the skuts of |'suds" from Ryans—I won't ever need naught
     else!

Ship me somewhere south of "Chi" though where the bloomin' mob
     ain't cursed
With a Volstead disposition and a man can quench his thirst
For the winter snows are falling and its there that I would be
Either Juarez or Havana with a widder on my knee!

* * *

Charley Wong

By H. A. D'Arcy.

The west was pretty wild when Bill Durant and I went out,
'Twer in '59 or '60, somewhar that about,
Bill took his pretty wife along (they'd been wed about a year),
A buxom kind of girl she war, that never thought o' fear.

And I don't know that she needed to, for the miners one and all,
Would have fought for her like devils if she'd ever made the call;
And afore we'd fairly built a hut to keep her from the damp
A little baby gal was born—the first one in the camp.

And didn't the boys keep Christmas? Well, I'm shoutin' now they
     did;
Why, they all got roarin' full that night just in honor o' the kid;
And by the time that baby were a little tot o' three years old,
She had a big tomato can just filled with virgin gold.

I built a cabin 'bout a quarter mile away from Bill's,
So we both had kinder cozy homes protected by the hills;
And Charley Wong, the Chinaman, had opened handy by
The laundry o' the canyon, and he washed for Bill and I.

Now, Chinamen ain't liked too well, and one day in a row
Charley got pretty badly used, I disremember now
Just what the trouble war about, but Bill war in the fray,
And he helped to beat the Chinaman in a rather brutal way.

Durant weren't bad at heart, ye know, but like too many others,
He didn't like Mongolians, nor own 'um men and brothers;
And I often heard him say that if the Chinamen wer near
He'd cut the leper's pigtail off and stick it through his ear.

One evening Lizzie (Durant's wife) and little Tot, the child,
Were comin' homeward down the hills when all at once a wild
And fearful howl were heard behind—two wolves were on their
    track,
Liz says she stopped and grabbed the child and threw it on her
    back.

Then shrieking aloud for help, she ran, as swift as any hind
Toward the Chinese laundry hut—the wolves came fast behind;
Nearer and nearer on they came; then reaching Charley's door,
The mother, with her precious load, fell prone upon the floor.

Bill and I were talkin' when we heard the fearful cries,
And rushing to the laundry the sight that met our eyes
Was far too horrible to tell, for thar was Charley Wong
Dead, and a blood-stained knife in hand full fifteen inches long.

He'd fought a fearful battle; one brute wer by his side
With its entrails all hanging out, and blood stains on its hide;
But t' other had got its work in afore Bill and I got there,
And wer gnawing Charley's throat and face till the bones were
    laying bare.

Wall, we made quick work o' Mr. Wolf, we filled 'um full o' lead,
Then gathered child and mother up and took 'em home to bed,
Next day when Lizzie told her tale, Bill's eyes were full o' tears,
He didn't brag much sentiment, and hadn't wept for years.

Poor "Washee!" when we packed him up the camp boys stood
    around
Each one with hat in hand and tearful eyes cast on the ground;
We shipped the corpse to 'Frisco, with a bag o' the yellow dust
To pay the freight to Pekin—to "Rest In Peace," I trust.

But ever after that, if any man had got the face
To say Chinese wer yellow dogs, he'd better quit the place;
For thar ain't a name more holy held in Canyon Idlewild
Than Charley Wong, the Chinaman, that saved Bill's wife and
    child.

*   *   *

A horse fly eats whip crackers.

The Song of Camille

Sitting alone by my window,
Watching the moonlit street,
Bending my head to listen,
To the well-known sound of your feet
I have been wondering darling
How I can bear the pain,
When I watch with sighs and tear-wet eyes,
And wait for your coming in vain.

For I know that the day approaches,
When your heart will tire of me,
When by door and gate I must watch and wait,
For a form I shall not see.
For the love that is now my heaven,
The kisses that make my life,
You will bestow on another,
And that other will be your wife.

You will grow weary of sinning,
Though you do not call it so
You will long for a love that is purer
Than the love that we two know,
God knows I love you dearly
With a passion strong as true,
But you will grow tired and leave me
Though I gave up all for you.

I was pure as the morning
When I first looked on your face,
I knew I could never reach you
In your high exalted place,
But I looked and loved and worshipped
As a flower might worship a star
And your eyes shown down upon me
And you seemed so far, so far.

And then? Well then you loved me
Loved me with all your heart,
But we could not stand at the altar
We were so far apart.
If a star should wed with a flower,
The star must drop from the sky
Or the flower in trying to reach it
Would droop on its stem and die.

But you said that you loved me darling,

And swore by the heavens above
That the Lord and all of his Angels
Would sanction and bless our love,
And I? I was weak, not wicked,
My love was as pure as true,
And sin itself seemed a virtue,
If only shared by you.

We have been happy together,
Though under the cloud of sin
But I know that the day approaches
When my chastening must begin,
You seem to think kindly of me
But you seem downhearted and blue,
But you will not always be
And I think I had better leave you.

I know my beauty is fading,
Sin furrows the fairest brow,
And I know your heart will weary,
Of the face you smile on now.
You will take a bride on your bosom,
After you turn from me,
You will sit with your wife in the **moon—light**
And hold your babe on your knee.

Oh! God I could not bear it,
I would my brain I know,
And while you love me dearly,
I think I had better go.
It is sweeter to feel my darling
And know as I fall asleep
That some would mourn me and miss me
That someone was left to weep.

Though to die as I should in the future,
To drop in the streets some day,
Unknown, unwept and forgotten,
After you passed me away.
Perhaps the blood of the Savior,
Can wash my garments clean,
Perchance I may drift on the water,
That flows in the pastures green.

Perchance we may meet in heaven,
And walk in the street above,
With nothing to grieve us or part us,
Since our sinning was all through love.

God says, love one another,
And down to the depths of Hell,
Well he sent the soul of a woman,
Because she loved—and fell.

And so in the moon-light he found her,
Or found her beautiful clay,
Lifeless and pallid as marble,
For the spirit had flown away.
The farewell words she had written,
She held to her cold white breast,
And the buried blade of a dagger,
Told how she had gone to rest.

* * *

To a Mountain Rat

By Frank B. Lindeman.

Yes I reckon God made ye
He's blamed for rattlesnakes,
And porcupines and woodchucks,
And if they ain't mistakes
Ye're a crowin' example
Of carelessness divine,
To nigh the danger line.

Yer winkless eye in innocence
Hides cunnin' cussedness,
And yer skin is full to bustin'
With a longin' to possess
All things that don't belong to you,
But when all's said and done
There's things on earth ye've failed to steal,
And reputation's one.

* * *

The real John Barleycorn of older days is gone, but not forgotten.

Those of us who knew him best, and loved him most,

Stuck with him 'til the last drop.

* * *

Pretty (looking over the new theatre downtown)—What do you think of the excavation?

Witty—Oh, it's pretty good as a whole.

The Bum and the Farmer's Son

One fine day, in the month of May, a dirty old bum came hiking; He sat down by a pig pen, which was very much to his liking. On the very same day, in the month of May, a farmer's son came piping; Said the bum to the son, "If you'll only come, I will show you things to your liking. I will show you the bees, and the cigarette trees, and the gum drop heights, where they give away kites, and the big rock candy mountains; And the lemonade springs, where the blue bird sings, and marbles made of crystal; you can whiff the breeze from the mince pie trees, where the wind blows fine and frisky; and you can join the band of Rocky Mountain Sam, and get yourself a sword and a pistol." The farmer's son then went along, listening to the bum's merry song; and for six months they did travel. Said the bum to the son, "When I get done, you're going to be a little devil." The punk looked up with his big blue eyes, and then he said to Sandy, "Now we've been a hiking all day long, now gosh darn where's your candy? You put a brace on my leg, and showed me how to beg, and you told me you were my jocker; and you told me lies, when you promised me pies, and you called me an apple knocker; I'm a goin' back home, no more to roam, I'm packing my junkerino; You can bet your lid, that this Hoosier kid, won't be any bum's punkerino."

* * *

Misplaced Eyebrow—"There is a hair in my soup."

Diplomatic Waiter—"Probably out of your mustache."

"I never thought of that."

* * *

Clap, Clap, Clap, Hurray!

"How do you like the Volstead Act?"

"I never did care for vaudeville."

Oh, the Merry Bells of Windsor

Johnny was late at school and explained that a wedding at his house was the cause of the delay.

"That's nice," replied teacher, "who gave the bride away?"

"Well," Johnny answered, "I could have, but I kept my mouth shut."

* * *

The Barb Wire Hairnet

Her has gone, her has went,
Her has left I all alone,
Can her never come to me,
Must me always go to she?
It can never was.

* * *

Some Parties, Ahoy!

"I suppose your wife was tickled to death at your raise in salary?"

"She will be."

"Haven't you told her yet?"

"No, I thought I would enjoy myself for a couple of weeks first."

* * *

Isaac Goldstein came home one evening, unexpectedly, and found a man sitting on his wife's lap.

Next day he told his business partner about it. His partner asked Mr. Goldstein what he had said to the man.

Goldstein replied, "I didn't even speak to him. He was a stranger."

Pasture Pot Pourri

Ashes to ashes and dust to dust,
If you don't like my figure,
Keep your hands off my shoulders.

* * *

Finishing Touches

"It's snow use," said Alvie; "we can't go tonight." And he hung up the receiver, while the fluffy flakes fell on the grass outside.

* * *

Jewish Bees

Biz-z _ _ _ Biz _ Biz _ ness.

* * *

"I'm through," cried Pedro, as he glanced over the Whiz Bang Winter Annual.

* * *

Tar Baby

I once knew
A Girl
Who was so modest
That she wouldn't
Even do
Improper Fractions.

* * *

Down in Dreamy Honohula

If I was a man in the land of orange and fig, I would sit with my thingamabob, and play on my thingamajig.

Longfellow
A tramp sat in the doorway of the box car, his feet dragging on the ground.

* * *

Strike Three!
They are fools who kiss and tell,
Thus it is the poet sings,
But that is why so many girls
Are sporting wedding rings.

* * *

SHE CREPT UP TO THE SCALES LIKE AN ARAB, AND SILENTLY STOLE A WEIGH.

* * *

Motto For Poets
If at first you don't succeed, keep on sucking till you do suck seed.

* * *

Mr. Martin of Martin's Ferry, protests against us writing our jokes on tissue paper so that our Philadelphia friend could see through them.

"Tearible," remarks Mr. Martin.

* * *

They are all roses, but some of them are pretty wild.

* * *

Will Be Dedicated By Request
What care we for Mary's lamb,
Now he's long been to sleep?
We'd rather see her pretty calves
Than those old, pesky sheep.

* * *

The cold weather chills me to the bone.
You should wear a hat.

Vengeance at Last

Suddenly there came a tapping as if someone were scrapping, slapping, rapping all the poets who write "Apologies to Poe"—just outside my chamber door.

*   *   *

Old Ben Jo' chewed slippery ellum;
Slippery ellum,
All the dern day long.

*   *   *

A Tough Break

Had a great tip on a horse yesterday called cigarette, but I didn't have enough tobaccer.

*   *   *

Da, Da, Daddy

I love them all, I love them all,
Please take me in swimmin'
With bowlegged women.
For I love them all.

*   *   *

"They sure soak you here," Gus remarked as he paid for a Turkish bath.

*   *   *

"How hoarse you are this morning."
"Yes, my husband got home very late last night."

*   *   *

My wife and I have been holding hands for twelve years. If we ever let go we'll kill one another.

*   *   *

My bride is a nice girl, but she sleeps with her knees up and the draft gives me a cold.

*   *   *

I'd like to see something in a lady's combination.

So would I.

We Found These Woids

"Why, honey, I love you with an equatorial passion that no adding machine can register."

* * *

Oregon Gal

There she goes on her toes,
All dressed up in her Sunday clothes,
Ain't she neat, ain't she sweet,
She has brand new stockings,
And nice big clumsy feet.

* * *

There are a lot of towns in this country that don't bury their dead. They just let 'em walk around.

* * *

Mr. and Mrs. Fish wish to announce the arrival of a couple of bouncing minnows.

* * *

Musicians have an easy job. While they're at work they're only playing.

* * *

I asked the boy across from my farm what he got for planting potatoes. He said, "I don't get nothin' when I do, but I get hell when I don't."

* * *

I got a fellow so drunk last night that it took three bell boys to put me to bed.

* * *

Wanted: Man to drive. Must bring hammer and nails.

* * *

Hey, Eddie!

Eddie was great at a party. In fact, you couldn't have a party without him. He was a great mixer.

Here It Is Again, Enlarged
Oh, Scissors, let us cut up!
Would Gillette me?

* * *

"I've come to the end of my rope," our hero cried as he threw his cigar away.

* * *

He mixed his beans with honey,
He'd done it all his life.
'Twas not because he liked the taste,
But it held them on his knife.

* * *

Teddy's Teachings
Get the habit, like the rabbit—multiply.

* * *

Let us all join in singing that timely melody:
"Keep her picture in your watch—you'll love her in time."

* * *

Going Up!
He started life as a chiropodist and worked his way up to be a throat specialist.

* * *

Don't always stand on the same side of the pulpit. You'll wear a hole in the carpet.

* * *

Here's to the girl that I kissed last
Who doesn't kiss slow and doesn't kiss fast,
With lips like a ruby and cheeks like a rose,
How many have kissed her God only knows.

* * *

"I'm the King of Siam!"
"Yesiam!"

* * *

He left the light burning so he could see to go asleep.

Oh the Moon Shines Bright

Look out lips, look out gums,
Look out tummy, here she comes.

*   *   *

Kentucky College

Bring on the "moon,"
Ring the bell,
Near-beer! Near-beer!
S.—O.—L.

*   *   *

The funniest thing I ever saw was a cross-eyed woman telling her hump-backed husband to walk straight home.

*   *   *

Mrs. Murphy asked for a nut cracker and her husband gave her a beer bottle.

*   *   *

The 1922 Girl

I should worry, I should care
I should marry a millionaire.
If he should die, I should cry,
I should marry my regular guy.

*   *   *

A little song entitled,
"OIL BY MYSELF"
By John D.

*   *   *

She's a wonderful girl. She can keep a secret in four different languages.

*   *   *

There is no difference between me and the prohibition agent. We're both after the same thing.

*   *   *

The moral of a dog's tail is that it invariably points to the past.

Wriggle Through This One

We have a terrible lot to be thankful for,
Now prohibition's here,
They've taken away our whisky, wines and lager beer,
They'll take away our tobacco next,
Along with the demon rum,
We'll have a deuce of a lot to be thankful for,
If they leave us chewing gum.

* * *

How Do You Get That Way?

A Jewish sergeant at Camp Lee in 1918 was explaining to a rookie the command, mark time, in the following manner: "Foist you raise yer right foot six inches in de air and then bring the left foot alongside the right one."

* * *

"Lovely day, don't you think," said the man as he hit his thumb with the hammer.

* * *

Two Swedes went to Ireland
To kiss the blarney stone,
But they couldn't catch their lutefisk
Where the River Shannon flows.

* * *

Willie, your face has changed quite a bit,
Yes, mother, dear, I've been washing it.

* * *

A change of wives ofttimes improves one's disposition.

* * *

Consolation

"Who is that terrible looking woman?"
"That's my sister."
"Oh, that's all right; you ought to see mine."

Dope This One

After Theophile returned to the city he wrote to Farmer Si Hopkins concerning a question which has been puzzling him for some time.

"Why," he inscribed, "do you lock up that donkey of yours so carefully every night?"

In due course of time came Farmer Hopkins' reply. "Because it is too good an *."

* * *

Hiawatha Skinned a Squirrel

Hiawatha skinned the squirrel,
  Just sat down and went and skinned it;
Went and skinned it to a finish,
  From its skin he made some mittens.
Made them with the outside inside,
  Made them with the inside outside,
Made them with the fur side inside,
  Made them with the skin side outside,
Made them with the warm side inside,
  Made them with the cold side outside.
Had he placed the fur side outside,
  Had he placed the skin side inside,
Had he placed the outside inside,
  And the inside inside
Then the warm side would have been outside,
  And the cold side inside,
So to get the fur side, warm side inside,
  Placed the skin side, inside, outside.
Now you know why Hiawatha placed the outside, fur side, warm
  side, inside, and the inside, skin side, cold side, outside.

* * *

For when the One Great Scorer comes to write against your name He writes not that you won or lost, but how you played the game.

* * *

"They don't look natural," said the man, as he rolled two threes.

How Kum?

Tom—"Where have you been for the last three hours?"

Bill—"In the saloon talking to the bartender."

Tom—"What did he say?"

Bill—"No."

* * *

Quick, Gents!

At sixteen, risque,
  Likes a naughty joke;
At seventeen, blase,
  Tries to learn to smoke;
At eighteen, mildish,
  Jolly just the same;
At nineteen, childish,
  Getting rather tame;
At twenty, breezy,
  Merely debonair;
At twenty-one, uneasy;
  So re-bobs her hair;
But when she reaches twenty two
  Her rush turns to a shove,
For then her motto has become:
  Love and let love.

* * *

Wanted: Man with ugly face to frighten children that play in my yard.

* * *

He Calls This "Poetry"

He's got a swell noodle,
Our friend Ted,
He wears an eight and a half hat,
For a six and a half head.

Dusting Off the Old Ones

Man went into German butcher shop and asked price of pork chops. To the reply of 30 cents a pound, he remonstrated that the butcher across the street asked only 20 cents.

"Why don't you buy them there, then?" asked the German.

"I would, but he's out," said the customer.

"Oh, vell, ven I'm oud, I sell 'em for only 10 sends a pound."

* * *

Eh, Maggie?

Here lie the bones of Peter Blunt
Down in this mothering nook.
Alas, he was too small a runt
To argue with a cook.

* * *

Warm Stuff

"My wife made it hot for me this morning."

"How was that?"

"I insisted on her getting up to build the fire."

* * *

My Advice

If you should marry a hootch hound
I'll tell you what to do.
Get a leaky boat and send afloat,
And paddle your own canoe.

* * *

Chicago Tribune's Column

(From the Charles City, Iowa, Press)

Manager Waterhouse, the movie man, who insists on giving his lady patrons the best, is improving the theater by renovating and decorating the ladies' parlor and lobby and ladies can—at least, feel that everything is fresh and orderly.

Classified Ads

This Soots Me

(From the Spokane Spokesman-Review)

YOUNG MAN, INDUSTRIOUS, WANTS to meet lady with enough cash to have her chimney swept. Dan Vail.

* * *

Whatcha Got?

(From Richmond, Va., Times Despatch)

HAVE four daughters; would like to put them in a business of their own. What have you to offer? P. O. Box 1092, City.

* * *

And Everything

(From The Duluth Herald)

I GOT 10 AKER of fine green timber dat I like for to sell on Miller Trunk Highway near Duluth. It bane yust vat yu want for a gude place to build cabin and have high old time, hunt yack rabbit & everything. I like for to go back to Norway & will sell very sheep. Write Lars Boguson, 1302 E. 8th St.

* * *

Ain't We Got Fun?

(From The Aberdeen World)

WANTED—Girl or lady to stay with me nights; room rent free. A–26, care of World.

* * *

The Wild and Woolly West

(From Casper, Wyo., Herald)

TO WHOM IT MAY CONCERN—In justice to my husband to quiet a few rumors to the effect that he had beaten me up, during our recent family trouble, is absolutely untrue. Signed, Mrs. Bessie Peters.

* * *

Jonah came from the whale with an awful cough.

The Busted Air Hose

An Italian was selling plaster of paris busts of great personages on the streets in New York. His cry was "Garibaldi, the greata man ina Italy, George Wash tha greata man ina United States. Tena centa each."

An American, thinking to have some fun with him, took one of his busts of Garibaldi, dropped it on the pavement and said, "To hell with your Garibaldi." The wop, not to be outdone, took one of his statues of Washington, threw it on the sidewalk, and said "To hell with your Georga Wash."

* * *

That Ought to Cool It

Jerry recently took Gwendoline for a ride in his new car and returned rather late. Approaching a steep hill he stopped the car, got out and raised the hood.

"What's the matter now," asked Gwen.

"I must cool the engine before I try to make that hill," replied Jerry.

"Oh, goodness alive," said Gwen, "It is getting so awfully late. Why don't you strip the gears?"

* * *

Tweet, Tweet

"I never spoke a cross word to my wife but once."

"Quite remarkable, that."

"Not so very. See that scar?"

How We Do It

A witty political candidate, after making a speech in an agricultural district, announced that he would be glad to answer any question that might be put to him.

A voice from the audience: "You seem to know a lot about a farmer's difficulties. May I ask you a question about a momentous one?"

"Certainly," replied the candidate, nervously.

"How can you tell a bad egg?" went on the merciless voice.

The candidate waited until the laughter had died down, then replied, "If I had anything to tell a bad egg I think I should break it gently."

He won the place.

* * *

April Fool!

It was only an old beer bottle,
Floating across the foam,
Just an old beer bottle,
Far away from home.
Only an old beer bottle,
With these sad words written on,
"Whoever finds this beer bottle,
Will find that the beer's all gone."

* * *

Another Married Chestnut

"I had a queer dream last night, my dear. I thought I saw another man running off with you."

"What did you say to him?"

"I asked him what he was running for."

For Men Only

When you play poker you take a chance; when you marry you have no chance.

* * *

Maids want nothing but husbands; after that they want everything.

* * *

Most of the women who cry at weddings have been married themselves.

* * *

Our Carpenter Hero

He "hammered" on the door; was answered by a girl who wore a white "sash," and asked if he could get a "square" meal. He "saw" that the place was "plane" but clean, and "planking" himself down to the table, he "braced" his legs beneath the chair, and "bit" into a Parker "House" roll. His "nails" were rather dirty, but he met the "stairs" of those about him with a "level" glance. After "bolting" his food, he "shingled" off a dollar bill, paid the girl, opining that it was a good place to "board."

* * *

The tenants who formerly lived on the floor above said that our baby balled them out.

* * *

Hi Say, Chappie

Maybelle (coquettishly)—You tickle me, Duke.

The Duke—My word, what a strange request!

Action vs. Words

Have you ever
After an evening
Of anticipation
Finally arrived
At the crucial moment
And with a
Depth breath
Taken the . . . . .
Initial step
Aeons later
A small voice
Somewhere is
Heard to say
"Don't"
While two arms
About one's neck
Refute the argument.

—Voo Doo.

* * *

Friday Special

Restaurant patron—Have you any whale, waiter?

No, sir.

Have you any shark?

No, sir.

Then give me a T bone steak. God knows I asked for fish.

* * *

"Waiter! There's a fly in my ice cream."

"Serves him right; let him freeze."

Our Rural Mail Box

Lou Z. Lizzie—I quite agree with you. A man who gives you his diamond ring to look at and then wants it back is no gentleman.

* * *

Mary Ellen Slapapple—The fact that your sweetheart gave you two black eyes is striking proof of his affection.

* * *

Howsh E. Shaykes—A change of pasture is good for the bull, you know, old dear.

* * *

Hittem Formy—Don't run your legs off after a woman; you'll need them to kick yourself.

* * *

True lovers never say good night until morning.

* * *

As a Rule

Clerk (at Employment Bureau)—"Someone has sent for a yardman, sir."

Manager—"We haven't any yardmen at present."

Clerk—"Then shall I send up three footmen, sir?"

The Barber Itch

Three prospective brides were in conference, Madge, Mary and Martha.

Madge—I am to marry a lawyer with fine practice. We are building a beautiful home.

Mary—My future husband is a banker and we will have a summer home, a maid and a car.

Martha—Well, girls, if you must know, I am to marry a barber.

Consternation reigned.

"What on earth are you going to marry a barber for?" gasped Madge and Mary.

Martha—Because any time a barber isn't kissing you he is talking about it.

* * *

A timid bachelor recently walked into a dance hall by mistake, and thought he was in a ladies' dressing room.

* * *

Jack—You certainly disgraced me at the banquet last night when you got drunk.

Jill—What did I do.

Jack—When the charlotte russe was served you tried to blow the foam off it.

* * *

Pee Ess

In conclusion, Gentle Readers, don't forget that Captain Billy's encyclopedia of humor and poetry, the Winter Annual, Pedigreed Follies of 1921-22, is awaiting you at your newsdealer or the publisher.

The Winter Annual

CONTENTS